Fairytales for Privileged Children

Fairytales for Privileged Children

Little Red Riding Hood Blows Her Trust Fund & Other Premium Tales

DANIEL FOXX

Illustrated by Axana Zasorina

monoray

First published in Great Britain in 2026 by Monoray, an imprint of
Octopus Publishing Group Ltd
Carmelite House
50 Victoria Embankment
London EC4Y 0DZ
www.octopusbooks.co.uk

An Hachette UK Company
www.hachette.co.uk

The authorised representative in the EEA is
Hachette Ireland, 8 Castlecourt Centre,
Dublin 15, D15 XTP3, Ireland (email: info@hbgi.ie)

Distributed in the US by Hachette Book Group
1290 Avenue of the Americas, 4th and 5th Floors
New York, NY 10104

Distributed in Canada by Canadian Manda Group
664 Annette St., Toronto, Ontario, Canada M6S 2C8

ISBN: 978-1-80096-387-0
eISBN: 978-1-80096-388-7

A CIP catalogue record for this book is available from the British Library.

Printed and bound in Great Britain

10 9 8 7 6 5 4 3 2 1

To Pret A Manger, without whom I would be nothing.

Thank you for everything you do.

"Are you living comfortably?

Then let us begin."

The Tales

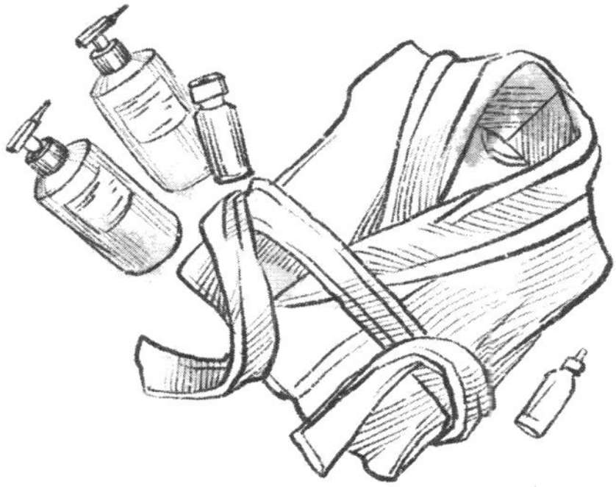

Little Red Riding Hood Blows Her Trust Fund

Once upon a time, there lived a very beautiful little girl who *loved* to shop.

She bought **bags**, and she bought **shoes**, and she bought **properties** in third world nations! It was lots of fun. She was especially fond of **outerwear** and frequently wore her signature Sophia-Loren-red cloak. Because of this, people called her Little Red Riding Hood!

One day, Little Red Riding Hood splurged a little too

hard on archival Chanel and completely decimated her trust fund.

"Whoops," she said.

"You must go and visit your grandmama," said Little Red Riding Hood's mother. "Bring her this hamper of titbits and preserves, and ask her to top you up a few mil. But remember: don't talk to any strangers!"

So off Little Red Riding Hood skipped, into the woods where her grandmama summered.

As she skipped, a wolf watched her. "I shall have this little girl for my supper," he said to himself, hungrily!

"Little girl," he said. "Where are you going with that basket of titbits and preserves— ahhhhhhh," he said, as Little Red Riding Hood pepper-sprayed his face.

"Oh, sorry!" said Little Red Riding Hood. "I thought you were a beggar! I'm taking this basket of titbits and preserves to my grandmama, who lives in a house in the woods."

"Which house?" said the wolf, through tears.

"...The **biggest** one, obviously," said Little Red Riding Hood, and she skipped happily on.

"I shall go to her grandmama's house and set a mighty

trap," said the wolf to himself, and he raced on ahead.

When Little Red Riding Hood got to Grandmama's house, she could see something was amiss! The gate was left open, and some of the staff weren't crying. **"She really must be ill,"** thought Little Red Riding Hood!

She went inside and found Grandmama sitting up in bed. It *looked* like Grandmama – she was wearing her

usual pearls and Hermes scarf – but something seemed different…

"Grandmama," said Little Red Riding Hood, cautiously. "I have brought you some titbits and preserves. But… oh! What pointy ***ears*** you have!"

"…All the better to *hear* you with, my dear," said Grandmama.

"But Grandmama," Little Red Riding Hood said. "What **BIG** ***eyes*** you have!"

"…All the better to *see* you with, my dear!" said Grandmama.

"But Grandmama," said Little Red Riding Hood. "What **BIG TEETH** you— oh no, pardon me, those are the veneers you had done in Singapore, and the upper blepharoplasty from Seoul. You are Grandmama after all. But did you not see a wolf come this way?"

"Oh, was that what I hit with my car earlier?" said Grandmama.

And they laughed and laughed and **laughed.**

Then Grandmama transferred a few million into Little Red Riding Hood's trust fund, and they all lived comfortably ever after.

Rumpelstiltskin

There once was a poor miller with a young daughter. To try and impress the king, the miller told him that his daughter could spin straw into gold.

"...But I can't spin straw into gold," said the miller's daughter, frowning. "And he'll obviously find that out pretty quickly and then punish you for lying to him. That feels like a really fundamental flaw in your plan."

"Oh," said the miller, who was presumably an idiot.

That night, the king locked the miller's daughter in a room full of straw and told her to spin it all into gold.

"Ugh, rustic, I guess?" said the miller's daughter, looking around the poky room. "But I still can't spin this nonsense."

Just at that moment, a funny little man appeared. He was three feet tall, with **long** ears and wild hair, and strange knobbly knees.

"Good evening!" he cried. "By my lucky pebbles three, I'll spin this straw to gold for ye!

But if this favour I should do

Something precious shall ye lose.

Lost forever this will be,

Unless you can guess my nam—"

"Rumpelstiltskin," said the miller's daughter.

"S… sorry?" said the little man.

"You're Rumpelstiltskin."

"How… how did you know that?" he said, deflated.

"You are literally the most Rumpelstiltskin-looking person

I have ever seen," said the girl, looking him up and down.

"Oh," he said.

"Get spinning, loser," said the girl, opening a copy of *Cosmopolitan* and putting her feet up.

As he spun, the girl had a thought.

"You know, we should E X P A N D ," she said.

"What do you mean?" said the little man.

"Well, instead of sitting here spinning single-handedly, you should teach other people to do it – in a third world country, perhaps. I'll be CEO, and you can be COO, and then we can both buy expensive carriages and castles, while other people do the work."

"That's a ***wonderful*** idea," said Rumpelstiltskin, and they went about inventing **CAPITALISM**. They hired pixies, and they paid them below minimum wage, and they set up a non-executive board. It was *lots* of fun!

Before long, MILLER-STILTSKIN & CO. was a **BOOMING SUCCESS.**

"Cheers!" cried the miller's daughter, clinking glasses with Rumpelstiltskin. "I have just finished buying up all the mills in town and forcing my father into financial ruin."

"How *fabulous*," said Rumpelstiltskin, taking a bump of caviar. "What shall we do next?"

"What else do billionaires do?" laughed the miller's daughter, waving her champagne. "We'll do a random trip to space, of course!"

"Of course!" cried Rumpelstiltskin.

And they clinked their glasses and lived comfortably ever after.

Sleeping Beauty

Once upon a time, there was a Princess called Viennetta. She was very beautiful and very rich.

"I'm so beautiful and so very rich," she yawned, waking up one morning. "I don't think I shall do anything today!"

"Won't you come down for breakfast, Viennetta?" enquired Nanny 3.

"No thank you," said Viennetta. "I've tasted everything worth trying already."

"What about some avocado toast?" suggested Nanny 3.

"Overdone," sighed Viennetta.

"…Granola?" tried Nanny 3.

"Passé," Viennetta replied.

"Eggs Benedict?" said Nanny 3, desperately.

"What is this, 1972?" said Viennetta. "No, I think I shall go back to sleep."

Later that day, Viennetta was still in bed!

“Viennetta,” called Papa. “Why don’t you get out of bed and play?”

“I could,” yawned Viennetta. “But I’ve already done everything worth doing. I’ve bought every pony and skied every slope. What more is there to do?”

“We could… go to Antigua?” suggested Papa.

“Oh, not Antigua *again*,” complained Viennetta.

“We could hire Taylor Swift for a private performance?” suggested Mama.

“Has she written anything new?” asked Viennetta.

"Well, yes, but it all sounds the same," said Mama.

"Then **no**," sighed Viennetta.

"We could go and throw coffee on a beggar?" suggested Nanny 3. "You like doing that?"

"Tempting," said Viennetta. "But I think I'll go back to sleep."

By this time, Mama, Papa and Nanny 3 were *so* worried about Viennetta they called a doctor.

"I'm afraid your daughter is simply ***too* comfortable**," said the doctor. "She is, in my professional opinion, chronically privileged."

"Oh my goodness," said Mama, proudly. "But is there anything we can do?"

"I do have an idea…" said the doctor.

Viennetta woke up with a start as Papa opened the door with a **BANG!**

"Oh Viennetta," he cried. "Come quick!"

"What is it?" she yawned.

"The government has taken all our money! We are ***poor!***"

With a scream, Viennetta leapt out of bed, her beautiful hair standing on end.

When Papa told her he was joking, they all laughed and laughed.

In the end, the only thing that could wake the Princess was her one true love: cash.

Hansel and Gretel

Once upon a time, two nice, privately educated twins were lost in the woods. Their names were Hansel and Gretel.

"Oh my gosh," said Gretel. "We're lost in the woods! Stepmama has taken the Land Rover Defender and left us all alone."

"I suppose she didn't want to share Papa's inheritance," sighed Hansel.

"Understandable," sighed Gretel.

They tucked in their Le Chameau wellingtons, tightened their Barbours, and set off into the forest.

As they walked, they became **hungrier** and **hungrier!** They hadn't eaten *anything* that morning, as Private Chef had been given a disciplinary for improperly muddling a panzanella.

Just as they were becoming *really* hungry, they came across a cottage made entirely of **candy & sweet treats**!

“Come, come!” said the old lady on the porch. “Taste my cottage of candy and sweet treats!”

“...Is that gingerbread?” asked Gretel.

“Why yes!” said the old lady.

“Is it store-bought?” asked Gretel.

“Y… yes?” said the old lady.

“No thank you,” said Gretel.

"How about one of my candy cane chimneys?

Or a toffee nut tile?" smiled the old lady.

"No thanks," said Gretel. "I'm doing keto."

"A sugar-swirl window?" said the witch, desperately.

"Is it coconut sugar or cane sugar?" asked Hansel.

"Cane—" said the witch.

"Oh dear," said Hansel.

"Perhaps a marshmallow doorknob—" began the witch

"Nothing tastes as good as skinny feels," said Gretel.

"Abs are made in the kitchen," agreed Hansel.

"Do you have some olives, or maybe a Huel?"

"I have gumdrop—"

"You and I both know those are riddled with

E-numbers," said Hansel, witheringly.

And with that, the witch went inside and

threw

herself

in

the

oven.

The Princess in the Tower

There once was a Princess who needed some me-time. Her name was Rapunzel, and she had beautiful long hair and was *very* stylish. Because of this, people were *constantly* asking for photographs with her – it was exhausting!

"Oh Mama," sighed Rapunzel, "I cannot even attend Atlantis Fashion Week without being *swarmed* by admirers!

I suppose I must have been cursed, to have such a symmetrical face and to be so naturally thin."

"Mmm..." said the Queen, who was busy writing suggestive poetry for Sir Lancelot.

So, one day, Rapunzel checked into the Four Seasons Albion for a much-needed break.

"I'll take the **Tower Suite**, please," she said.

"With the—"

"With the dragon concierge, yes," she clipped.

She and the dragon had lots of fun! They did Korean face masks, and watched **RuPaul's** *Dragon Race*, and read VOGUE *Camelot*.

"Look!" said Rapunzel. "This suit of armour is best for accentuating a narrow waist."

"Snatched!" agreed the dragon.

It was *great* to do a digital detox. However, just as Rapunzel was starting to feel rejuvenated, a handsome Prince appeared at the base of her tower.

"Rapunzel, Rapunzel," he cried. "Let down your hair!"

"...Sorry *what*?" said Rapunzel.

"Let down your hair and I will climb up and rescue you!" he called.

"...I'm reading *Let Them*," she snapped. "*Please* go away!"

And he went away.

The next day, he came back once more!

"Rapunzel, Rapunzel," he called once more.

"Let down your hair!"

"Oh my gosh," she said. "How am I *ever* going to get a minute of peace?"

"I have an idea," said the dragon – and they cut Rapunzel's hair into a fierce little bob.

"There!" she said, looking chic as hell. "Now you *can't* climb up!"

And the Prince went away for another night.

The next day, he was back *again!*

"Rapunzel, Rapunzel, maybe you could tie some sheets together or something—" he began.

"Oh my goodness, this is ridiculous," snapped Rapunzel, nodding to the dragon. "Go on then."

And the dragon swooped down and gobbled up the Prince in one go.

"Girl dinner!" giggled Rapunzel and the dragon, and they snuggled up to browse TikTok.

Humpty Dumpty Sues for Damages

Humpty Dumpty sat on a wall,
Humpty Dumpty had a great fall.

All the King's horses and all the King's men
Couldn't put Humpty together again.

Humpty Dumpty had to go private,
He paid for an air ambulance and its pilot.

He saw a consultant, and a physio as well,

Who managed, with time, to repair Humpty's shell.

Humpty's mother, The Rt. Hon. Dumpty,

Was a high-profile lawyer who worked in the city.

She drew up a case and, backed by her firm,

Sued the King and sent him their terms.

"Why was there no **CAUTION** *sign on the wall?*

Was a safety assessment conducted at all?"

"Why was no medical expertise called in first,

Rather than ALL the king's horses *and an* army,

who quite obviously made everything worse?"

"I, uh— we didn't think—" said the King.

"No, you *didn't* think," said The Rt. Hon. Helen Dumpty, **slamming** her hand down on the courtroom desk. "You demonstrated a *complete* lack of oversight as an employer and owner of a wall, very nearly leading to a bright, promising young egg losing his life – or at the very least, sustaining life-altering injuries. And it is for *that* reason, your Honour, that we are suing for £40 million in damages – to cover medical costs, loss of future earnings, and psychological damage."

"Agreed," said the judge.

Humpty Dumpty sat on a wall.

Humpty Dumpty moved to *Dubai* in the fall.

The Princess and the Low Thread Count

There once was a Prince who was *desperate* to marry a Princess.

He rode all around the kingdom, and he threw a hundred balls, and he signed up to Raya – but no matter how hard he looked, he just couldn't find a real one!

"Everybody *calls* themselves a Princess," he cried, "but they're all *nouveau riche* at best!"

"Trash, the lot of them," slurred the Queen Mother, who was drunk but in a rich way. "It's Meghan Markle all over again!"

That night, there was a **BIG SCARY STORM**. As they sat in the drawing room, they heard a great **BANGING** on the palace doors!

When they all rushed to look, they found a girl standing there, sodden with rain. She had water dripping down her balayage and sloshing out of her The Row flats.

"Will you please help me?" asked the girl. "I am a Princess, but I have been caught in the storm! May I stay at your palace for the night?"

Now, the Prince and the Queen Mother were immediately suspicious: why would a "Princess" be walking alone in the rain? But the girl explained that she had been *pretending* to take a walk for a PR opp and got lost, which made sense.

So, they welcomed her in and put her up for the night. But the Queen Mother had a cunning plan.

Whilst the servants prepared a bedroom for the girl, the Queen Mother sent one of the maids to Tesco for an own-brand bedsheet. She instructed this to be placed over the mattress.

The next morning, the Princess did not come down to breakfast.

When they opened the door to her chambers, they found her **stone-cold dead**, lying atop the mattress.

"Alas, she was a true princess," nodded the Queen Mother, sadly. "For she could not touch a polyester blend and live."

And the Prince sought out the girl's Royal family, and married one of her sisters. And they lived comfortably ever after.

The Three Bears and the Home Invader

"Wake up, Rupert!" called Mama Bear, tapping on the mid-century teak staircase. "It's time for breakfast."

"Coming, Mama," called Rupert, springing from his medium-firm mattress and pulling a Massimo Dutti knit over his ears.

It was another lovely day in the woods: the leaves were falling, the birds were s i n g i n g, and the

Duke and Duchess of Sussex were filming content in the neighbouring chalet.

"What would you like for breakfast, Rupert?" murmured Papa Bear, who was busy reading *The Telegraph*. "I for one am having porridge."

Rupert took a taste of his Papa's porridge. Yuck!

"These oats aren't steel-cut!" he gasped, scraping his tongue. "They won't nurture my microbiome!"

"How about my granola, Rupert?" asked Mama Bear.

Rupert took a taste of Mama Bear's granola. Ouch!

"This granola is *too* healthy!" he said, spitting out a tooth.

Mama Bear shrugged. She was an almond mum.

"I know," Rupert said. "I'll have some of my special *overnight* oats. They've got added marine collagen, which will be good for my future FINE LINES and wrinkles."

"Excellent idea," said Mama Bear.

"It's giving Gwyneth Paltrow," murmured Papa Bear, who had now moved on to *The Spectator*.

So Rupert sat in his Eames chair and endured his breakfast.

Later that morning, the whole family headed to the annual Teddy Bears' Picnic. It was lots of fun! Mama brought her crustless quiche, which everyone agreed was elegant but understated, and Rupert read one of his poems about post-industrial decline. Then Papa committed a faux paw, forgetting that Winnie and Baloo had recently separated.

"How was I supposed to know," he hissed to Mama, who was drying Winnie's tears. "I can't keep up with those two and their breakups!"

All in all, it was a successful picnic. However, when the trio got home, they found the front *door* ajar!

"Someone's sat in our chairs," cried Papa, looking at the improperly chopped cushions.

"And someone's eaten our breakfasts," cried Mama, looking at the empty refrigerator.

"And *someone's* in my bed!" cried Rupert, staring at the blonde girl in his bedroom.

"Ahhh, three bears!" screamed the girl upon waking – which Rupert thought was quite impudent, actually, given she was in their house.

"Ahhh, what terrible roots!" he snapped back, eyeing her dismal bleach job.

Thankfully, Mama had already called the police, and the girl was quickly escorted to a young offender institution.

And the Three Bears pressed charges, and they lived happily ever after.

The Easter Bunny's Career Change

The Easter Bunny went hop, hop, hop!

He gave chocolate eggs to all the children in the land.

He gave a chocolate egg to Jennifer, and a chocolate egg to Thomas. But when he tried to give a chocolate egg to Rupert, he would not take it!

"I think I would prefer a chopped salad," said Rupert.

"Or perhaps some GREEK yoghurt. It's better for my glycemic index."

The Easter Bunny sighed, for he had always hated giving out chocolate.

"The truth is, I never wanted to be a chocolate bunny," he confessed to Rupert. "I actually went to Oxford."

"Well, why don't you retrain?" said Rupert, poking at the chocolate eggs in his basket. "Are these even single origin?"

"No," sighed the Easter Bunny, ashamed.

So that night, the Easter Bunny went home and made some changes. He phoned some friends, and called in some favours, and wrote up his CV.

The next day, all the children cheered and waved to see the Easter Bunny again – but he ignored them.

"Sorry, no time to chat," said the Easter Bunny. "I've pivoted into finance."

The Easter Bunny loved his new job! He hopped all around the office, doing important tasks.

Hop, hop, hop! He fired Jen from accounts.

Hop, hop, hop! He embezzled funds.

Hop, hop, hop! He expensed a flight to the Maldives.

Eventually, the Easter Bunny became *so* successful, he was known as "The Bunny of Wall Street". He divorced

his wife, and started dating the New Year's Guinea Pig, and took prescription medication with the Krampus. It was a lot of fun!

But as the Easter Bunny's empire grew, the power went to his head!

Hop, hop, hop! He mis-sold PPI.

Hop, hop, hop! He caused a housing bubble.

Hop, hop, hop! He tipped the economy into a recession.

"Whoops," said the Easter Bunny.

Everyone was *very* angry with him! They shouted, and waved their arms, and stamped their feet, and took away all his lovely money.

"However will I afford my lifestyle now?" sighed the Easter Bunny, sadly.

"I have an idea," came a voice behind him. Turning round, he saw a lady all in white. She had white hair, and a white catsuit, and big white sunglasses. It was the *Tooth Fairy!*

"I propose an alliance," she said.

"*You* double your chocolate output, and *I'll* cut you in on the extra teeth I get as a result."

"Like a cartel?" said the Easter Bunny, thoughtfully.

"*Exactly* like a cartel," smiled the *Tooth Fairy*.

And so the Easter Bunny went back to delivering his chocolate eggs – but this time, he did it with a smile.

Because now, he was an *entrepreneur*.

The Pied Piper

Once upon a time, the upmarket residents of Hamelin had a rat problem.

"This simply will not do!" they cried.

"It's bringing down our market value!"

So, they sent word far and wide for someone who could rid them of their wretched rats.

"These accursed rats are nibbling at our hampers and

fromages!" they said. "We will pay a great sum of money to anyone who can stop them."

Eventually, a mysterious gentleman arrived, dressed in strange colourful clothing.

"My goodness, is that LOUIS VUITTON?" enquired a woman.

"Vintage GUCCI," explained the man.

"Ah," said the woman.

At this, the man started to play his pipe, and all the rats followed him out of town! He led them to a river, where the rats jumped in and drowned.

When he returned, the residents of Hamelin were appalled.

"Okay, firstly, that was animal cruelty," said one woman.

"And secondly," said another, "you have just filled our river with rats. That is gross. We are not **paying you**."

The Piper was furious! He vowed to get revenge.

The next day, he returned to the town and approached one of the residents' children.

"Hello little girl— AHHHHHHHHH," he said, as she pepper-sprayed him in the face.

"Sorry," the girl explained. "I don't talk to beggars."

"I'm not a beggar," shrieked the piper, wiping his eyes. "I'm trying to get paid for my rat thing!"

"Oh," said the little girl. "Well, I don't talk to the help either – try someone else."

And she went inside.

Next, the Piper approached a little boy. He began to play his strange tune to lure the little boy away. As if in a trance, the child began to walk towards the piper… and then straight past him. He was wearing Bang & Olufsen noise-cancelling headphones, and could not hear a thing the Piper was doing.

Cursing, the Piper tried **ANOTHER** little girl, sitting all on her own outside a café.

He took out his pipe and began to play his haunting tune. The girl watched him, transfixed. Then she cocked her head.

"Is that Sabrina Carpenter?" she asked.

"What? N— no," said the Piper. "It's a Magic Tune—"

"I liked her second album, but I can't say I've listened much to the third. Can you do Addison Rae?" she said.

"No," faltered the Piper.

"What about K-pop?"

"I can do Celine Dion?" said the Piper, desperately.

"Who?" said the girl.

And the Piper marched straight out of town and

hurled
himself
into
the
river.

Snow White's Near Miss

Once upon a time, in a land far, far away, there lived a beautiful Princess. She had hair as black as coal, and lips as red as roses, and skin as pure and white as snow – because she maintained a rigorous twelve-step Korean skincare routine. People called her Snow White.

Snow White had a very fabulous stepmother, the Queen – who, like many women over forty, dabbled in the occasional bit of witchcraft.

Every day, the Queen would look in her magical mirror and ask "Mirror Mirror, on the wall, who's the fairest of them all?"

And the mirror would say, "You are the fairest of all, my Queen."

However, as Snow White grew older, her beauty shone more and more brightly. And one day, when the Queen consulted the mirror, its answer had **changed!**

"It is *Snow White* who is most fair, my Queen," it said.

Snow White overheard this and knew the Queen would be *very* upset.

"Oh, my poor stepmother," she said. "She does yoga, HIIT *and* Reformer, and hasn't eaten a carb since 1346. I wouldn't blame her if she wanted to murder me!"

So, Snow White decided to leave home, and headed into the enchanted forest. There, she came across a quaint little cottage, which was home to seven little men!

Their names were Skinny and **Bratty**,

Wealthy and CLASSY,

Fruity and GIVENCHY

and **Nepo**baby,

and they welcomed Snow White into their home.

"Hi, ho!" they said.

"Your skin is flawless, so you can stay with us for as long as you like."

They had lots of fun in the cottage! They sang funny songs, and plaited each other's beards, and watched *Real Housewives of Neverland.*

However, it wasn't long before the Queen discovered where Snow White was hiding.

She put on a disguise and scuttled up to the cottage with a basket of **poison apples!**

"Would you like an apple, my dear?" she smiled, offering the basket to Snow White.

"Oh, no thank you," said Snow White. "Fruit is full of sugar."

The Queen sighed, because she knew that Snow White was right. "You are quite right. I have taught you well," she said. "But I am afraid because you are fairer than me, I do now have to murder you."

"I understand," said Snow White. "Go ahead."

But as the Queen raised her dagger, Skinny had an idea!

"Wait," he said. "Can we just check something quickly?"

So they returned to the castle, and they all stood before the magical mirror.

"Mirror, mirror, on the wall," said the Queen. "Who's the fairest of them all?"

"It is still **Snow White** who is most fair," said the mirror.

"*But,*" said Skinny, who had been admiring the Queen's outfit this whole time. "Who's the biggest ***slay*** of all?"

"Oh, undoubtedly that is the Queen," said the mirror. "She's giving *mother*, slay the house down, snatched to the gods, fierce and sickening."

"Am I really?" asked the Queen, her eyes welling up with tears.

"Oh, one hundred per cent diva," said the dwarves enthusiastically.

And with the reassurance of multiple little gay men, the Queen relaxed, and she and Snow White returned to being the best of friends, and they nudged the wealthy king towards an early grave.

Jack and the Non-Organic Beanstalk

Once upon a time, there lived a young boy called Jack and his mother. They were land rich but cash poor, as his mother's assets were tied up in some crucial long-term investments at that particular time.

One day, Jack's mother told him to go to the market to sell their cow, as they needed the money and she had also read that dairy wasn't "in" anymore.

"Farewell, Mama," cried Jack, pulling on his Moncler puffer. "I shall go to the market, and come back with some money to save us!"

However, when Jack got to the market, he found himself face to face with a curious man. He told Jack that he would take his cow, in exchange for some very *special* beans.

"What's special about them?" asked Jack, cautiously.

"They were featured in *goop*," said the man.

"Oh! Then I will take the lot," said Jack eagerly.

When Jack got home and showed his mother the beans, she **GASPED!**

"Oh my goodness, Jack, you swapped our cow for these *beans*!?" she exclaimed, holding her face. "What an *excellent* idea. I *adore* legumes."

So she took the beans and made a cassoulet, and sprinkled the remaining beans in the garden.

The next day, there was *quite* the surprise. A gigantic beanstalk had grown in the garden!

"Oh, Jack…" murmured Mama in horror. "I don't think those beans were organic!"

Jack climbed the beanstalk – he **climbed** and **climbed** until he reached the top, where he found a huge cottage.

Inside, there was a large table, spread decadently with picky bits. Jack had never seen such a wonderful assortment of *amuse-bouches*! But just as he was about to help himself, the ground started shaking.

A giant was entering the room!

"Fee, fi, fo, fum!" came a loud voice.

"I smell the blood of an Englishman…

and it's got a *wonderful, sumptuous* sort of

copperiness to it that I *just* love!"

It was Nigella Lawson.

Hurriedly, Jack swiped an **enormous** can of ***Perelló*** olives and a bucket of Fortnum's caviar, and made a break for the door – but Nigella spotted him.

"Fee, fi, fo, fum!" she called, giving chase.

"I'll put you in my *microwavé*!"

Jack *dashed* down the beanstalk –

but when he got to

the bottom,

he realised Nigella Lawson was following

him! His mother tried to chop the beanstalk down

with an axe, but she hadn't been to Reformer lately,

and her arms had lost some of their tone.

Before they knew it, Nigella was in their garden,

towering
over them.

"Fee, fi, fo, fum!" she screamed.

"You took my hummus and my olives…

but you forgot a good crusty loaf

to pair them with."

And she pulled some bread out of her pocket and laid out a fabulous spread in the garden.

Then Mama popped a good bottle of Margaux, and they all lived happily ever after.

The Three Little Pigs and the Big Bad Tenant

Once upon a time, there were three little pigs. Their names were André, Stèphen and Stephan, and they owned a portfolio of properties.

One day, a big, scary *wolf* came prowling around.

"Little pigs, little pigs," he began. "Let me in to your—"

"Do you have a booking?" said the first pig, **slamming** open the door. The wolf was taken aback.

"No?" he said.

"Ugh," said the first pig. "We *might* be able to squeeze you in. Are you a cash buyer?"

"What? I don't—" began the wolf.

"Come on, come on, we don't have all day," snapped André, and they ushered him inside.

"Is this house made of straw?" the wolf asked, baffled.

"Um, it's thatch, you dumb b*tch,"

said Stèphen, sipping a martini. "It's cottagecore."

"Yeah, it's giving *Evermore-The-Holiday-Practical-Magic*," said Stephan, filing his trotters.

"Tbh we're airbnb-ing this, so you can't live here," they said, and steered him towards a house made of sticks.

The wolf looked at the house. "This house is made of sti—"

"First of all, it's mahogany," said the second pig. "And it's a chalet, not a house. Perfect for après-ski."

"We're actually doing après-ski right now, but you can't join, Elton didn't bring enough raclette."

"Who's Elton?" said the wolf.

"Elton John," said the pigs in unison. "Our dear friend."

Next, they drove to a house made of bricks.

"This one is 800,000," said the third pig.

"No onward chain."

"I— I can't afford that!" stammered the wolf! "Why, I should huff and puff and blow this house down!"

"Good luck Wim-Hofing a house made of bricks," said the third pig. "No… you can rent. We will need six months' deposit up front and a guarantor."

"Bills not included," said André.

"That's almost my entire salary!" said the wolf, sweating.

"Try spending less on coffee," called Elton, from the G-Wagon.

"Is that black mould?" panicked the wolf.

"No," lied Stèphen. And they set off for Mykonos, and lived happily ever after.

The Two Ugly Sisters

Once upon a time, in a far-away kingdom, there were two sisters. Their names were Porchetta and Frankette. They were known for their wonderful senses of humour – unlike their stepsister Cinderella, who was drab and boring and didn't like to gossip.

Some people said Cinderella was extremely beautiful, but in a tacky, obvious way.

"She's *off the rack* beautiful," said Porchetta, reassuringly. "We're beautiful in a *runway*, editorial sense."

"Yes, that's right," said Frankette. "When people call us the 'Ugly Sisters', they mean it in a chic, **Berlin vibe**."

Porchetta and Frankette tried *very* hard to be kind to Cinderella. They called her affectionate nicknames, like "Pig Girl" and "Stinky Susan", and they gave her advice on how to style her rags. Their mother – Cinderella's stepmother – even allowed her to stay in the house after Cinderella's father took an unfortunate

fall

down

the

stairs.

But despite all of this, Cinderella still didn't seem to like them!

One day, the Prince announced a grand ball, to which every young maiden in the land was invited.

"I shall wear my Balenciaga," said Porchetta.

"And I shall wear my McQueen!" said Frankette.

"What shall I wear?"

said Cinderella,

popping her head out

of her bin.

"Oh, Cinderella," said Frankette sadly. "I think you had better stay home. Self-care is important, and you have *so* many chores to get through. Don't overload yourself!"

"We're just thinking of your mental health," said Porchetta, kindly.

And they headed off to the palace.

Everyone had *lots* of fun at the ball! The sisters ate little cakes, and whispered about Thumbelina's outfit, and threw it back to some instrumental harp music.

Then, just as it was their turn to dance with the Prince, who should arrive but Cinderella! She was wearing a big puffy dress, with a tiara and glass slippers.

"Well, *she* looks *extremely* new money," said Porchetta.

"Whereas *we* look very 'David Rose'," said Frankette, admiring their angular gowns.

Strangely, the Prince enjoyed dancing with Cinderella all evening – until, at the stroke of midnight,

she fled from the ballroom,

leaving only one of her horrible glass slippers behind.

"I must find the girl who can wear this slipper," cried the Prince. "And then marry her!"

"Right, screw this," said Frankette. "We're going to Turkey."

A couple of weeks later, the sisters returned to the kingdom. Porchetta had treated herself to a deep-plane facelift, while Frankette had new veneers and a **BBL**. They looked absolutely gorgeous.

When the Prince called at their house, he immediately forgot about Cinderella, and brought the two caked-up sisters to meet the King and Queen.

"I suppose the moral of *this* story is that no one's ugly – they've just not spent enough money yet!" laughed the girls through their frozen lips.

And they married the Prince and his sister, and lived happily ever after. And Cinderella remained in her bin.

Beauty and the Beast

Once upon a time, there was a girl called Belle. She was very beautiful, and very smart, but she lived in a tiny rural town – and not in a Cotswolds way.

Belle liked to walk around the streets and sing little songs.

"Oh, poor me. I am special because I can read, and yet I have to live in this dumb shithole town," she sang. "Oh look, there goes the ugly baker, doing his lame stinky job again."

Everyone loved Belle!

One day, Belle's father became lost in the woods, and was taken prisoner by a **BIG SCARY BEAST!**

When Belle heard this, she immediately set off to rescue him.

"Please, let my father go!" cried Belle, knocking at the gates of the castle.

"Never," said the Beast. "He will have to stay here with me, a terrifying beast, in my 800,000 square feet countryside property."

"Did you say 800,000 square feet?" said Belle, blinking.

So, Belle agreed to take her father's place, and began to settle into her new home.

She had lots of fun at the castle! She was served *haute cuisine*, and took selfies in the rose garden, and chatted with the furniture.

"I don't suppose there's a Mrs Dyson Airwrap wandering around anywhere, is there?" she asked, hopefully.

"I'm afraid not," said a chair. "But we do have a Miss BaByliss?"

"Oh," said Belle, sadly.

As time went by, Belle and the Beast began to get to know each other better.

They liked the same books, and the same paintings, and they both agreed that they would sooner die than own an Android phone.

"Here's a fun game," said Mr Diptyque Candlestick. "Why don't you count to three, and both say something you *hate?*"

"Okay!" said Belle.

"One... two... three..."

"Inheritance tax!" they both cried.

And how they laughed!

"Oh, Beast," said Belle. "Whyever do you not have a wife?"

"I wish I did," sighed the Beast. "But who could ever marry a big, scary, 6'4" Prince like me?"

"...Sorry, did you say Prince?" said Belle, salivating.

Before long, they were happily married. And with her

newfound wealth, Belle gentrified her old village, and forced the original residents out, and replaced the baker with a Gail's.

And they lived comfortably ever after.

Little Red Riding Hood's Birthday Party

"Wake up, Grandmama!" cried Little Red Riding Hood. "It's my birthday!"

"Happy Birthday, Little Red Riding Hood," whispered Grandmama, who still had stitches from her recent facelift.

It was Little Red Riding Hood's big day, and she was *very* excited. She put on a new red cloak, and her favourite wolf-fur stole, and Nanny 4 made her an egg white omelette.

"You can have the yolks, if you like!" Little Red Riding Hood said to Nanny 4, kindly. "I know you don't care about your **weight**."

Soon the guests started arriving for Little Red Riding Hood's big birthday party. She *loved* birthday parties!

Hansel and Gretel arrived first, along with two of Little Red Riding Hood's friends from boarding school, Passata and Crouton.

They put out decorations, and liaised with catering, and organised drinks for the guests.

"Now, Little Red Riding Hood," said Grandmama sternly.

LRRH

"As you are only ten years old today, you cannot drink hard liquor. Please stick to white wine."

"Yes, Grandmama," said Little Red Riding Hood solemnly, taking a glass of crémant.

Soon the guests were arriving – and everyone in the enchanted forest had come! There was Snow White, and Belle and her new husband, and the fairies, and the blind mice, and even Sleeping Beauty – though she quickly reclined on the chaise longue.

Everyone had *lots* of fun! They played games, and gossiped, and took turns bullying the Ugly Duckling. The Two Formerly-Ugly Sisters compared surgeons with

Grandmama, and The Little Mermaid splashed around in the champagne fountain.

Then they ate the Muffin Man!

"Ahhh, help, I *make* muffins, I'm not *made* of muffins!" said the Muffin Man.

Everyone thought that was very funny!

Just when Little Red Riding Hood thought her party couldn't get any better, there was a wonderful surprise. Her uncles, the Three Little Pigs, popped in on their way to Sitges!

"Darling, happy birthday!" they cried. "We brought you a set of Tiffany lamps and a mid-century farmhouse table."

"Just what every ten-year-old girl needs!" gasped Little Red Riding Hood.

"Now remember," said her uncles, as they headed back out the door. "Next time, don't *kill* your wolves – charge them rent instead!"

And everyone smiled and nodded, for they had learned a valuable lesson that day.

Mrs Claus Comes to Town

"She's coming, she's coming!" cried the children, throwing on their Boden pyjamas. "Mrs Claus is coming!"

"Don't you mean Father Christmas?" puzzled Nanny 2.

"*No*," scoffed the children, rolling their eyes. "Father Christmas does the *normal* children. Mrs Claus deals with the *comfortable* children, like us!"

It was Christmas Eve, and everyone was *very* excited. They had drunk their evening espressos, and instructed Nannies 2 and 3 to decorate the tree, and then watched *A Christmas Carol* – a horror film about a man called **Scrooge**, who is bullied for being fiscally responsible.

"We must put out her favourite drink," said Casper, placing a Vesper Martini on the mantelpiece.

"And a snack, in case she's hungry!" said Sephora, carefully selecting three almonds.

Then they rushed up to their bedrooms, and fell asleep as fast as they could!

Some hours later, there was a gentle clip-clop outside. This was, of course, not the sound of hooves – but of Mrs Claus's heels as she stepped out of her traditional BENTLEY Continental.

Mrs Claus did not *slide down the* chimney. Instead, she carefully stepped through the letterbox, which she was able to do because she used to be a model and was still watching her figure.

She t i p t o e d into the house, quiet as a kitten.
It is said that Mrs Claus knows the layout of every house in Richmond – and lo and behold, she knew *exactly* which wing of the house the sitting room was in!
She is very magical.

She knocked back her martini and munched half an almond, and then – with a mysterious smile! – she reached into her Birkin and began pulling out presents for all the children…

Soon their stockings were full to the brim, and quick as a flash, Mrs Claus was back through the letterbox and drink-driving to the next abode, barely swerving at *all*.

"She's been!" cried the children the next morning. "We knew she would come!"

"What has she brought, children?" smiled Mama, cradling her morning wine.

"I've got Everton Football Club!" said Casper, excitedly.

"And I've got a Tracey Emin!" said Sephora.

Mrs Claus had even left something for Mama and Papa!

"A syringe of Mounjaro,
how kind!" gasped Mama.

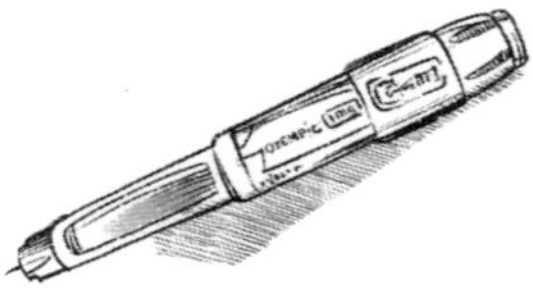

"What did she leave you, Papa?" enquired the children.

"Her number," said Papa, looking down at the perfumed paper.

"That's Mrs Claus!" everyone exclaimed.

And they chuckled wealthily.

The Dragon's Day Off

The dragon was bored.

He flew around the tower – flap flap flap – and he did a big roar – roaaaaar! – and he immolated a knight – SIZZLE!

But every night, the dragon dreamed of more.
He dreamed of New York Fashion Week.

So, one day, the dragon packed up some of his treasure,

and said to the wicked witch, "I would like to take some annual leave."

"Have a nice **holibobs**!" said the witch.

The dragon flapped his big wings and flew all across the kingdom.

He flew over the enchanted forest, and past the royal castle, and eventually landed in Manhattan.

At first, everyone was very scared of the dragon! They screamed and ran, and refused to give him directions.

The dragon was very sad. However, just as he was about to give up and fly home, he heard a voice.

"I like your wings – is that patent leather?"

Looking down, he saw a small woman with a bob and sunglasses. It was Editor-in-Chief of *Vogue*, ANNA WINTOUR!

"You know, people call *me* a dragon," she said. "I like to think it's a compliment."

From then on, they were the best of friends.

First, she took the dragon shopping. "You must have a hat," said Anna Wintour. "Everyone has a hat!"

The dragon felt very splendid in his new hat.

Then, they went to a grand hotel.

"You must stay at The Mark," she said. "Everyone stays at The Mark!"

"Ahhhhhhohmygodwhatisthat, ahhhhhhhh,"

said the receptionist.

But when they saw Anna Wintour, and the dragon's suitcase of treasure, they soon brightened up.

"This way, Mr Dragón," they cried, showing him to a suite.

The dragon and Anna Wintour had a pillow fight!

Then they went for lunch.

"You must eat at Balthazar," Anna Wintour said. "Everyone eats at Balthazar!"

They had steak frites, and a crisp sparkling water. The dragon felt chic!

However, when they went to see some runways, there was quite a commotion.

"Excuse me," said an angry woman behind the dragon. "I cannot see the models for your big dumb hat!"

The dragon felt very silly. He took his hat off.

"I think I should leave," whispered the dragon.

"You could," whispered Anna Wintour.

"Or you could kill her."

Anna Wintour was very wise!

The show began, and everyone settled in to watch the models.

"The draping is *impressive*," said the dragon, munching on a leg, "but it's no Schiaparelli!"

Everyone found that *very* funny. The dragon was the toast of fashionable society!

Soon, it was time for the dragon to go home.

"Oh Dragon," said Anna Wintour. "Please don't go. Your wings are too beautiful and your takes are too polished – you must stay in New York and be my Creative Director!"

"Oh Anna Wintour, I wish I could – but then who would guard the **Witch's Tower**?" the dragon cried.

"Can't she just get a Ring doorbell?" said Anna Wintour.

So the dragon pivoted into publishing, and bought a townhouse, and lived happily ever after.

And they all lived comfortably ever after.

DANIEL FOXX is an award-winning comedian and writer from London, described by *Rolling Stone* as "utterly hilarious and effortlessly charismatic".

Online, Daniel's comedy videos have amassed millions of views and over a million followers. His viral sketch series “Bedtime Stories for Privileged Children” went on to be published as a collection of tales in 2024, and this book is the sequel.

Daniel writes for stage and screen, with his hit show *Unfortunate: The Untold Story of Ursula the Sea Witch* touring internationally and earning him a Writers’ Guild Award nomination.

Daniel has appeared on BBC One, BBC Three, ITV and Comedy Central, and has written for the BAFTA-winning series *Late Night Lycett*. He wrote and starred in two series of BBC Radio 4’s *POV*, and co-hosts the smash-hit podcast *Welcome to Hell* with Dane Buckley.

This monoray book was crafted and published by Jake Lingwood, Mala Sanghera-Warren, Alex Stetter, Emily Campbell, Rachael Shone, Jeremy Tilston and Caroline Alberti.